Great A Gain
Version of the
Nation

Vol 2

Frank J. Hiri

DEDICATION

To those who inspired me in this!

CONTENTS

ACKNOWLEDGMENTS

My interest in writing of this book was sparked and fostered through my distinguished students, teachers, professors, and friends. My special thanks go to a friend, Pamela Foland, the author of Megan's World Book series who helped me in configuration of this book with editor and its publisher.

Preface

Great A Gain. Version of The Nation" is the next collection of facts and theories to convey a greater standard of comforts and conveniences to the American lifestyle. The chapters in this book are neither intended for political nor theological propaganda. The author believes the learned knowledge of a person is the product of humankind and academia inspirations that, should be shared upon. A unique aspect of this book is the irrelatively between its chapters while each is enduring perpetuity

and each being **A Great Gain** for its audience readers. However, should there exist any transcendence, the readers of a greater critical views are invited to compromise perceptions in a greater standard of the lifestyle so to stand informed of the current events within the completion of this then the next volumes.

- A **flip Over** of **privacy perception in marriage life** is a new Gain for the human chapter.
- A beginning of an era for the human beings to take **control over the earth movement in the space is discussed for a better orbit and presented with <u>a fact that the earth movement is a product of the atmosphere movement in the space to carry this planet</u> thus, known <u>as the Earth Consequential Movement caused by the Space Force Resistant while the Atmosphere is pushing up.</u>** (Vol.1)
- A **Retroactive and Retrospective Oil and Gas** theory to justify The<u> **World Division of the Oil.**</u>
- The chapter eight discusses a **Partial Crime Con**
  - **trol Strategy** but untouched to the Second Amendment.

    • The role expectancy of each person is an interesting chapter to read.

1.
LOVE AND/OR THE COMMITMENT

DEFINITION
THIS DEFINITION TO APPLY ONLY PRIOR
TO ESTABLISHMENT OF RELATIONSHIPS

LOVE IS A SELF-MOTIVATED NOTION,
EXERCISES A DESIRE TO INFLUENCE POWER-
AFFECTION
PERIODIC, CULTURAL AND SEEKS SELF-
SATISFACTION,
WHEN IT RESTS AND REGARDS NO COMMITMENT,
ITS VALUE DIMINISHES TO COUNT DOWN SHOULD IF A
TRUSTLESS

ITS PRIMARY* PURPOSE (WHETHER OR NOT TWO
SIDED) STANDS TO SUPPORT ONLY ONE SIDE, (THE
SELF) WHILE THE SECONDARY* SIMULTANEOUSLY
FOLLOWS A LOGIC/LESS AFFECTION THOUGH NOT A
CIRCUMVENT.

AMONG ALL THE NOTIONS AND MEMBERS OF A
PERSON,
IT'S THE ONLY NOTION THAT,
NEVER TAKES THE BRAIN ORDER AT THE FIRST PLACE
PRIOR TO ITS AUTO- HEART REFERRAL.
THEREFORE,
CAUTION PREREQUISITE IS A MUST!

THE SEQUENCES OF ITS RELATED TRANSACTIONS TO
FOLLOW WHEN,

1) THE EYES TO VISUAL AN INTERESTING, BEAUTY
   OR HANDSOME PERSPECTIVE OF THE OTHER
   SIDE.

2) OTHER SIDE IS NOT THAT MUCH OF INTEREST BUT AN INTERVENING INTEREST, A-LIKED-SOUND OF A MUSIC CIRCUMVENTS THE POSITION
3) IT ACTS AS A TIME OR MOOD SEEKER

THEN,

THE COMMUNICATIVE **ELECTRO-CHEMICAL DOTS** OF THE BLOOD REFLECTS, PULSING TO **SAVE** THAT **PERSPECTIVE** DIRECTLY INTO THE HEART, WHERE AN ALREADY PREREQUISITE-ROLE-EXPECTANCIES EXISTS TO OPT OUT ANY TO WHOM IT NEVER LIKES.

HERE, THE PERSON SHOULD BE PROFESSIONAL ENOUGH TO THEN, SEEK

AN ELECTRO-BRAIN REFERRAL, NOT LETTING THE **LOGIC-LESS** HEART TO **BE CONQURED** BY THE ABOVE THREE SEQUENCES HOWEVER,

SHOULD EVER THIS TO HAPPEN,
THEN, THE FOLLOWING IS A MUST!

THE COMMITMENT

WHAT IS THE COMMITMENT?

PENDING UPON EACH PERSON'S PERCEPTION, THE COMMITMENT TO INCUR WHEN,

1) THE LOGIC/LESS LOVE ENDS TO A MARRIAGE,

2) A CHILD IS BORN,

3) A JOB IS ASSIGNED,

4) A CIRCUMSTANTIAL ATTACHMENT IS CREATED

5) <u>A DUTY IS DELEGATED</u>

<u>AND SO ON</u>….

NOT YET REACHED THE DEFINITION!

IS THAT AN AGREEMENT OF PARTIES INVOLVED?

NO, NO!

IT IS NOT A TWO-SIDED DECISION

WHILE BEING OF

ONE OF EACH TO INVOLVE, AND A DUTY OF WHICH

INDIVIDUALLY, IS A SELF-BURDEN.

A COMMITMENT TO BECOME TWO SIDED WHEN ITS VALIDITY TO REACH A *SOLID* DECISION OF EACH PARTY TOWARDS THE PURPOSE INTENDED FOR THE LIFE OF THE PURPOSE AND THE ENFORCEMENT TO WHICH **PRUDENTIALLY OPINIATED** TO BE A MORAL-CONTRACT **THUS, LEGALLY FASHIONED** (NOT A BUSINESS CONTRACT).

THE EFFECT AND LEGALITY OF LOVE AND THE COMMITMENT WITHIN THE UNDERLINED DEFINITION:

SADLY, NEITHER LOVE NOR COMMITMENT ARE CONSIDERED TO BE RANKED AS AMONG THE LEGAL PRESTIGIOUS ISSUES.

WHEN LOVE TO INCUR PRIOR TO THE ESTABLISHMENT OF RELATIONSHIP, IT IS
PERSONAL, AND
PRIVATE,
SO, IT DESERVES BE ENRICHED BY ANY AND ALL THE PRIVACY LAWS.
HERE IS A SAD PHILOSOPHY SUPPORTING A THIRD-PARTY GROUPS, THE OTHER SIDE OF THE ISSUE, KNOWN TO BE (THE OPPORTUNISTS) WHO ADVICE
"TO OUT-LOUD YOUR LOVE"
AND THEIR CIRCUMVENTIVE REASONING STANDS TO IDENTIFY
THE PUBLIC AS PROTECTIVE SHIELD TO THE LOVE-CARRIER (THE PERSON IN LOVE) BUT, NOT THE PRUDENTIAL
HOWEVER, THEIR ACTUAL INTENTIONS
ARE NOTHING LESS THAN:

1) TO INTRUDE THE PRIVACY OF THE LOVE-HOLDERS
2) POLITICAL IMPOSITION
3) CULTURAL IMPOSITION
4) ABUSIVE DISORDERS

SOMETIMES THEIR ACTS AMOUNT
BEYOND A SIMPLE PRIVACY INTRUSION.

HERE, THE DUTY OF A PROPER LEGAL SYSTEM SHOULD FUNCTION,
1) TO DISCOVER THEN, SEEKING A PUNITIVE DAMAGE OF THIS GROUP.
2) ADVISING THE LOVE-HOLDERS OF CERTAIN AGES
(ABOVE 13 OR TBD BY THE CONGRESS) TO AVOID OUT-LAUDING, TO AVOID SHARING YOUR LOVE STORY WITH ANY-ONE(EXCEPT CLOSE FRIENDS AND RELATIVES), AND **EVEN TO AVOID**

SHARING YOUR LOVE WITH THE OTHER SIDE PRIOR TO THE ESTABLISHMENT OF SO CALLED, THE RELATIONSHIP BECAUSE THE LOVE IS PRIVATE, IT IS A SELF-MOTIVATED NOTION SO, HAS TO BE MANAGED BY SELF AND THE EASIER WAY IS CONVERSION FROM THE HEART TO BE SURRENDERED BY THE BRAIN.

3) THEN, ADVISING THE LESSER THAN THIS AGE GROUPS TO HAVE THEIR **BLOOD*** RELATED RELATIVES ADVICE WHILE THE AFFECTION'S CONNECTION WITH THE HEART VARIES TO ALL THE MENTIONED CIRCUMSTANCES INCLUDING THE **CONDITION OF THEIR BLOOD*** WITHIN THE AFFECTION PERIOD

EFFECT:

1) THE LOVE PRIVACY PROTECTION LAW DEMINISHES THE RATE OF TEENAGE PRAGNANCIES.
2) THIS LAW TO ALIGN AND NORMALIZE THE INTRUDERS ACTION AT LARGE AS WELL AS THEIR PERCEPTIONS.
3) PUNITIVE TO DEFEAT THE POLITIC
4) ANY AND ALL PRIOR MARRIAGES THAT WERE DEFEATED BY OUT-LOUD CIRCUMVENTIVE OF ENVIRONMENTAL SHALL SHAPE TO STAND WITHIN THE NORM AND PRIVACY OF ONLY TWO PERSONS, HUSBAND AND WIFE, PROVIDED NOT TO EXCEED THE SCOPE OF RELATIVES AND THE ALREADY PERFORMED MARRIAGE AUDIENCE.

2.
THE LEFT BEHIND ELEMENT OF
A MAJOR PREVENTIVE RELIEF ON
CORONA VIRUS,
THE THREE TIMES A DAY USE OF THE
TOILET *

...Due to a fact that the most of a person's sicknesses are associated with his or her <u>Stomach</u> because the most effective medicines are consumed by <u>the Stomach</u>...

<u>If you clean your Stomach by USING THE RESTROOM TREE TIMES A DAY</u>

<u>by any means; keep it smooth, Drinking Water, Juices, Exercise and or even sometimes by taking light Laxatives if is needed then,</u>

<u>YOU ARE LESS LIKELY EVER BECOME SICK!</u>

This means; the viruses and bacteria of any kinds are **OUT** prior to occupy cells in the stomach, the primary place then, the secondary, elsewhere should the person to miss hand washing, face touching, and sneeze catching.

EFFECT: This time I shall leave the drawings of all effects to the audience readers, and I'm pleased to add the following question before a few of them who're only involved with the related practice and professions.

Q… If at all the above idea to make a sense, then **would a colonoscopy to credence an infected patient among with the actual related preliminary and the general treatment?**

The content of this chapter was referenced from chapter 11

3.
THE PRIVACY PERCEPTION IN MARRIAGE LIFE

The **privacy-perception** in marriage life while being within a diversity cultural range has most of the time been misconstrued causing an increase in the divorce rate (a catastrophe in general) specially in the recent decades!
Here, if it's asked of the <u>definition of the privacy within the scope of the marriage life,</u> the most answers we would get are, "each husband and wife should respect the privacy of each other ".
Thought, all these responds are being an establishment of professional opinions like the marriage consultants, it seems <u>disgraceful</u> to any innocent <u>marriage-life.</u>
Here, the author introduces a **fact*** to correct all prior misperceptions upon analytical on both, the definition, and the actual functional risk mitigation strategies of privacy perception in marriage life.

The **<u>TOTAL</u> CONSENSUAL PRIVACY INTRUSION**

<u>in all aspects of life by husband and wife together would reduce the Divorce Rate*</u>

<u>provided to be recorded in the marriage contract or strongly agreed by the married couples.</u>

Why should the human beings to live with fantasy-perceptions within their marriage life while their actual intention to marry is an establishment of a **UNITY*** (rather than united against **) [regardless of a disgrace fact that our history and laws have always weighty been an advocate of the divorce**rather than marriage* upon a framework of an Individual Right **influenced by cultural diversity**].

The **unity** of both shall support to defeat and supersede (a monster) to be known as each unit, husband, or wife who separately each were united with their prior sided-family and friends and during years and strength all of whom are supported by the next one sided-monster, the legal divorce advocate and industry **among its business power.

Now,
if the actual intention is a solid marriage, when **each husband or wife to sacrifice their privacy and reshape it to a combined-single-privacy capable to defeat environmental hostile then, the actual hardship of life would size to ease.** And the only remaining issue is the alignment of the two separate privates to a single perception.

A conversion in legal divorce industry** (the supply) to another substitute job industry also shall diminish* the divorce rate among the couples (the demand).

EFFECT: The Lifetime marriage is what we always wanted!

4.

A PROTECTIVE NATIONAL RIGHT OF CANADA

- It's the Mid. January 2020, <u>The Move.</u> of Harry and Meghan of UK to Canada.

- It appears they've intended for a persona comfort purpose thought the followings

  should always be a precaution to the world thus, the Canadian:

- The rise of Southwest Left Wing enriched and fueled by Southeast

  Left Wing in decades, The pleasure and pressure of which the later often

  became an intrusion.

- Today the Left so disparate with a wrong fueled power while lacking a capitalistic capability, they would do anything to take away the rights of the Right.

- Princess Diana of UK has never been a leftist, while an advocate beyond a recognized loyalty to a right royal wing.

- Thought her advocacy was not a product to cause her death, it sounds it enriched her son, the former prince, the move. to evident this, a lack of loyalty to a powerful right wing! It's OK for persona comfort!

- Then,

  The young generations change their mind all the times:

  IS THIS A GENERATION THE NEXT POLITIC?

  THE SENERIO TO FOLLOW:

  - It is the 2030, The Prince William, if the king,

  - The brothers to acquire **An Extended Regional Power** claiming Harry and Meghan as the

    new Duck and Duchess of the UK's Canada, while the land on stake.

    EFFECT: The author's question from his audience readers is whether a question before the Triangle and the Queen should be now! or Harry and Meghan's Royal contract is of a Separation Perpetual.

5.
BABIES LEG ALIGNMENT

On or around the walking ages, heavier babies on their earlier walking stags place too much of their body weights burdened on their legs consequentially not to gain a normal leg-beauty that otherwise they should have gained when they grew up. The question calls the parents of whom if an option
of delay in baby's walking may be available? The Parents choices to consult with a professional health care during the entire period of baby's walking would credence. Also, a normal delay on walking commencement shall secure an ultimate shape of the baby's legs. It's of course a possibility that, the food selections within this period would be an element essential to gain the purpose intended.

EFFECT: Health and beauty fulfilment.

6.
RIGHT AND LEFT SIDED CHEWERS

Obviously under the age of forty the most of people may have never noticed of their habitual status whether if being **Left or right-Side-Oriented-Chewers** while eating. When if they ever notice this, should they start to change to the other side to secure the balance in **strength and the health of their teeth?**

7.
THE GREENLAND

It's the August of 2019 and schools have already started. The news media reveals that the US. Government is interested in purchasing Greenland. Giving a point view in the following

the author's best Legal Analysis is presented for the readers of this chapter:

The Greenland <u>Real Property</u> may be **offered** for purchase or sale (by a buyer or a seller) and By

a) The US. Government
b) A US. State Government
c) A US. citizen or entity with the US Supreme Court's approval (a <u>jurisdiction</u> supportive to if any further case dispute may incur).
However, the entire Greenland local government alone or along with all the discretions of the Danish government dominant to the Greenland are considered being the **unique** <u>**Intellectual Properties Vested Remainder**</u> <u>**for the Life in the present and future Nations of**</u> <u>**Greenland and**</u> cannot at any time be divested by any contract, court, or law. Therefore, any Denmark's and otherwise contracts for sale or purchase aren't solidly binding and they are

voidable but not void (analogy to a contract with a minor/s).

However, should such an indefinite vested remainder only be divested by an attachment or will of its nation to be sold, yet it is only (a right transformation by the current will of the nation of the Greenland if by a referendum) thus it is valid only for the life of their <u>Current</u> Generation therefore,

Reserving the next generation's right
    under the

Rule Against Perpetuity

Now, if the US, one of its state, entity, or one of its citizens to purchase the same from Denmark or Danish government they legally would have Nothing more than what the Danish government or its local government has now!

EFFECT: Greenland and or any world's land that included (attached) with a nation and formed with a governing structure thus, equipped with an Intellectual Property of Non-Divestiture Nature always reserving their next generation's Rule Against Perpetuity.

8.
A PARTIAL CRIME CONTROL STRATEGY UNTOUCHED TO THE SECOND AMENDMENT

Isn't it better without blaming the second amendment of our Constitutional Right, the blamers if any, each to submit to an appropriate entity or agency a Creative Offer, a <u>Partial Crime</u> <u>Control</u> <u>Strategy</u> in a micro-capacity of their perception to align and meet to conform with the macro-level Strategical Rule of our Laws in a coordination with the Second Amendment to satisfy the **best interest** of the Nation and the Government then, abroad?

The author

here is submitting his share in a partial Crime Control Strategy:

The last Saturday of the August this year, the 2019 a shooter guns down seven and injures twenty. Considering his motivation, it was told that, **he was fired** by his <u>employer</u> and while complaining the matter to the state and the FBI, he accidently was stopped by a police officer for a minor traffic violation. This time he has opened fire to the officer then, the people presumably with a pre-meditated act (while having prior sets of guns in his car).

The Author's share:
The following
Regulation for Employers
may help
To Control some of related Crimes.

THE NEW REGULATION TO FOLLOW:
The employers shall <u>strictly </u>be liable (for <u>Contributory Negligence</u>) for not having an <u>Informed-Reminder</u> form signed by the employees immediately one minute prior to the firing of the employees of their rights to file <u>Unemployment-Benefit</u> <u>including Food Stamp</u>.

<u>EFFECTS: This may prevent creation of a Heat of Passion, an element in criminal intent.</u>

9.
A BIG LOTTERY TO WIN

One of the interesting issues among all discussions with a friend was a question that I was faced when spending sometimes with, on the August of 2019,

Asking

"What would you do if you win a big lottery?"

The following was an intuitive respond that sounds to be the reflective of that, specific friend who has inspired me

Isn't it best to ask,

'WHAT WOULDN'T YOU DO when you win a big lottery?

EFFECT: The Wealth not to Influence the diverse natures.

10.
CLIMATE CHANGE THEORY

To consider the above title while regarding it to any unsuitable condition on our environment in <u>different weathering time zone</u> the author introduces the following statement inviting his audience readers to the following scientific analysis in oppose to a political one but, not limited to the rights and privacies.

"Any and all past human efforts to construe the climate changes may be considered in analogy with mother nature product of a **FIVE-MINUTE RAIN** that, **CLEANS-UP** the entire environment **IN   A SECOND** <u>for the life of being</u>, the duration of that specific **CLIMATE BUILT UP** and after each   cleans up.

While either side believers must respect the opposition opinions including consideration of a fact that,

<u>a large, accumulated employment over the life of the climate control is created in this industry being in stake therefore,</u>

WITHOUT A SUBSTITUTE EMPLOYMENT

all the transactions of either sides in reduction of the climate control change in funds without the above consideration sounds unreasonable thought the essential substitution of the climate control employment changes should legally be vested in our private and public sector expertise then,

Perhaps the new **Space Force Industry** would be a proper size for a large partial employment replacement.

EFFECT: Clear perceptions and opinions of my audience readers on this chapter may produce a valuable **clue**.

11.
GENERAL HEALTH AND THE RESTROOM

In this chapter the author hereby introduces a very valuable **opinion** of his personal physician, the practice and the result of what always has been effective then, it lends to credence the at large!

The **Opinion** reads,

......**Due to a fact that, the most of a person's sicknesses are associated with his or her <u>Stomach</u> and the most effected medicines are consumed by the <u>Stomach therefore,</u>**

<u>If you keep your Stomach Clean by</u>

<u>Using the Restroom Three Times a Day you less likely become sick!</u>

Effects: General Health

12.
POSSIBLE FLIGHT CRASH PREVENTION

Researchers on the past runway flight crashes regard departures as well as arrivals. Rivers and lakes are the ordinary preventatives that were projected for the purpose on the runway ends in the past as an effective experience.

If at all not yet been experimented, dose it worth to use the **Beach soil** for the purpose intended? If so, is there any remedy experimental should the soil being **wet** on the rainy days then, would it result to a lesser, best, or not at all any effect?

EFFECTS: National and International Safety and Security

13.
BILL AND CAPITALISM

Study shows that, the past generations in the United States have produced bills as large as five grands and in the market.

Now, to generate the Eco.Mec.Cap, a Capital Economic Mechanism
to
insure and secure
part in economic value of dollar

Long being yet we haven't had a taste to test this!

The important question may arise if the large bill production in our current era would
be helpful to the Economy v. Security deficiencies?

Can the public and private sectors together to vote decreasing their notions of accountability should such an experiment to show a potential result.

EFFECT: The effect shall follow to Experiment this Practice.

14.
NECK LEANING

Based on the people habitual sleeping figures, the weight of their heads and or other related criteria **they** more often are categorized as **RIGHT OR LEFT SIDED NECK LEANERS.**
This may in a health configuration effort be normalized by an exercise of balancing to reduce the area-related- muscle pains.
The following example shall clarify this

Watching a TV program for a long time while your siting position being not in your proper straight visual line with the tv, and you're forced to lean either left or right on your neck causing pain. Therefore, A proper line of watching a TV is **a Straight Line**.

EFFECT: Consequential pain relief to the area muscles.

15.
POLITIC IS WHAT WE DO, BUT NOT WHO WE ARE

What the author has asserted on his preface page reads ...the chapters in this book are neither intended for political nor theological propaganda...

Here, his reader audience may ask, quote but what about the title of this chapter?

Despite any and all other chapters in this book, the title of **this chapter is not the author's belonging nor he represent this title** he instead has selected it of a sounded media and he has an strong/specific interest to brake this title down for his audience-readers how should they judge when they're faced with such an statement in an English literacy deceptively arranged to influence them or with **such a wrong grammatic statement unacceptable to the legal world** !

Thereafter, <u>why and how</u> should they be aware of **<u>a</u> <u>false suitability</u> on such a kind of statement intending to misrepresent possibly to defraud them as follow:**

- The two irrelevant short statements of "politic is what we do" but, "not who we are" while, each separately being a correct sentence are wrongfully combined intending to shape a compound sentence by an added transitional phrase of" "but" which <u>was wrongfully abused to</u> combine these two sentences to shape one statement of a desired outcome, to exonerate the maker of the statement.

- Here, this shows an obvious intent of the writer of this statement nothing less than showing <u>a false-suitability</u> to his/her readers-audience.

- Beside should ever the compatibility of the two words of "politics" and "who" be considered in terms of comparing, the two words are needed to be within a single parameter of a one related scope while "who" is of a <u>person</u> and "politics" being of a <u>subject</u> that, can't be compared or contrasted with two different categorical words.

- Also, the word of "politic" in a point view of a reasonable prudent-perception shall be defined but not limited to <u>a bad but, a good politic</u>.

Here, the statement reveals that, the writer has a prior intention to limit it to a "bad politic" excluding "good ones" because it was desired an exoneration quote "not who we are".

- The only remaining considerable fact could be as the writer/s have no intention to defraud or misrepresent while having **no clue** of what were done (written) was wrong. Then if so, such an act is excusable by law.

Furthermore, this statement is not supportive of any legal academician should if to be introduced to a court of law, it would have not been admissible as evidence because it is an "asked and answered" statement of one party intending to answer a prerequisite question of …do you do politic?...

16.
RETROACTIVE AND RETROSPECTIVE OIL & GAS LAW OF <u>INTERNATIONAL RELATION</u> , A PRACTICIBLE THEORY

THE THEORY

IN ADDITION TO THE INTELECTUAL PROPERTIES THE CONSTRUCTIONS OF ANY AND ALL OIL AND GASS PRODUCTION AND REFINERIES A <u>CAPABLE COUNTRY</u>* HAS BUILT (OR TO BUILD) ON A LAND OF AN INCAPABLE COUNTRY THEN, IMMEDIATELY BEEN CONVERTED AND BECOME THE

INTELLECTUAL PROPERTY, THAT OF
THE CAPABLE COUNTRY WITH
A VESTED REMAINDER RIGHT FOR
LIFE, BEING THE LIFE OF THE
CONSTRUCTION, INDIVESTABLE
THOUGHT
THE EVER-RIGHT OF <u>**USAGE AND**</u>
<u>**ENJOIMENT**</u> **BEING THAT OF THE**
INCAPABLE ONE.
THE CAPABLE'S ARBITRARY
EXPARTE WILL OF A GOOD CAUSE
SHALL SUPERSEDE TO EXERCISE A
DEMOLITION OR THE SALE OF
SUCH INTELECTUAL PROPERTY TO
A THIRD PARTY IN EXCHANGE
WITH US. DEFICITS
AND WITHOUT ADJUDICATION BY
THE UN. AND OR OTHERWISE.
THIS LAW TO APPLY TO ANY
NUCLEAR AS WELL AND SPACE
FACALETIES.

THE HISTORY

- Several countries are inherited with an underground possession of reservoirs since their birth, a time existed no professional production skill to be used.

- Should this <u>era</u> be considered a commencement to constitute an

Ownership Right of such reservoirs

when then, existed no **Contract Law** at the age **industrial revolution**

Thought both,

- The following ownership are to be the ones of the **most values**:

(1) Moral Ownership:

- A prudential definition for a **Moral Ownership** stands to protect the rights of

countries lacking any reservoir on expense of all reservoir possessors provided the extend of decisional discretion to be shifted only on possessors with a **Total Independent Production Capability*** to secure all contracts of sales with countries lacking a reservoir as well those with but lacking production capabilities.

- The popular definition of **Moral Ownership** regards any reasonable perception   to the simple term

existentialism for the countries lacking a reservoir.

(2) Legal Ownership Even though the legal ownership of these reservoirs is presumed to   belong to their birth-inherited respective countries but, **the ability to use and production** of which lends not to credence **an absolute legal ownership** for each specific possessor after the age of the **industrial revolution** unless such a country possesses a **total independent production capability*** such as the United States of America and or some other European countries.

EFFECT: Is it reasonable now to claim that   **a big burden** was shifted to the capable **nations**   Thus, **resulting many loses for them** to enrich others since the industrial revolution, the starting of oil and gas production. Therefore, **THIS THEORY converts any and all real properties, the constructions and refineries of incapable countries to an INTELECTUAL PROPERTY OF capable country (the constructor) , a life time vested ownership being the life of the constructions and the refineries.**

*TOTAL INEDEPENDENT PRODUCTION CAPABELITY carry a capability if there existed no production facility and no refinery on the land at all. **Any and all constructions and facilities made in the shape of real property for the production purpose by such a capable country remains the life time vested remainder right of such a capable country while an unlimited possession and USE of the production of that constructions and facilities being a right of incapable country then it can be divested by an arbitrary exparte will of the capable for a cause without any adjudication by UN or otherwise.**

17.
KNEE HELTH

A requirement to secure the proper use of our knees while we possess a seating- job calls attentions to use an <u>appropriate chair.</u>
Here a choice is the one that the height of the seating portion of the chair to be exactly equal to the size of the person's leg from the bottom of the feet to the knee. This shall create a pressure resistance preventive to the knee.

18.
BRAIN'S REAL FOOD

First, it's good to be reminded that, the brain is the server of all functional computing component members of the human body without which all functions are impossible. Therefore, the brain food is the primary element to keep the members going,

So far, dose the same food we eat feeds the brain too?

The answer sounds being correct but, our state of thoughts, mentality, the intellectual intelligence and so on....... probably are needing additional and different kinds of food!

Yes, this, **the secondary Brain Feeding**

differs in each person based upon their state and levels of work, knowledge, experience, age, origin, nationality and much more………

The **Sources** of such feedings range from **reading, thinking, listening, learning, practicum, involvement**, and more……

all of which lends in <u>protection and grew</u> of the brain in a matter of which are related to the

person's above practice involvements.

You may even need not to spend any effort to feed your brain a simple example is when you're in front of a shelf of electronic shop or a grocery store your **<u>scrutiny to a device</u>**
or
<u>ingredient of a food</u> yet feeds your brain.

19.
SKYDIVING

With all the developments including the new added
Space Force to our branches of
Armed Forces this young force is yet concerned
with the upper level of its hierarchy.

it's easy to start **the theoretical education** from the
elementary and high schools that forms

the **beginner mindset** <u>essential</u> then,

the practice to proceed a higher encouragement like
Skydiving Facility in one in each city's chosen
high school.

Effect: I trust if we use this young industry to
develop up in both ways, up and down would be the
best ever grown industry.

20.
CEILING FAN

The ceiling fan's primary **usage** being **a change in the condition of the air** now is extending a change in **the quality** of the air too.

An experimental study reveals a fact that in the rural or even urban areas the usage of ceiling fan after about each two months on any season has the following **qualitative** effect in addition to its primary intended purpose being a change in the **condition** of the air:

TICK PILE OF DUSTS
appears attached around the blades rising a health issue where **is needed** to be cleaned by a few **wet cloth or paper towel,** the dust that we used to breath

This shall rise a **secondary question** whether it is **Possible or practicable to build a Removable Filter around the edge of the ceiling fan blades?**

EFFECT: Increase in Average Age.

21.
EACH PERSON'S ROLE EXPECTANCY
WITHIN THE NATIONAL SCOPE
THEN, THE GOVERNMENT

It's obvious that each government requires its
nation to obey each individually the laws that they
assign,
known as the **Government Role Expectancy**. this
is involved with criteria* structured and disciplined
over <u>thousand years</u>.

Here comes now whether the **Nation's Role
Expectancy** of their government is under any
<u>criteria*</u>
and are they disciplined by......?

Obviously, people with their individual capacity
have role expectancies that, sounds being of an
individual thought thus, not prudent.
often their expectation goes beyond the norm while
it is reflective of their faith (being of the individual
desire) then, creates a conflict that, diminishes their
comfort zone.
The following tips are given to identify some of
these criteria:

- When a crime happens towards a person's relative the role expectancy of such a person of the government sometimes goes beyond the norm requesting a **warranty** to justify their lose
- But the actual duty of the police department should be "**doing the best as they're capable of and equipped with under circumstances**" yet the person insists a warranty to justify!

Individual role expectancies towards their government have never been qualitative as the Government role expectancy since the individuals have never been organized well!

22.

THE RIGHT TO VOTE, A THEORETICAL REVISION TO THE 1978 CONSTITUTIONAL AMENDMENT

It's on or around April & May of the 2019 and within the advocacy scope of the first 2020 presidential primary election almost all the front runners of the Party Democrat nominees are asserting a right to vote for criminals ranging from the terrorists to murderers, rapists, and......finally to the Illegal Immigrants. The fact is unknown as to whether this advocacy is an essential path of the democrat campaign and belief or It's only an assertive revenge-shield to the opponent party. Here the author submits the following theories that may be a good remedy for prudential consideration:

• Terrorists to resume their constitutional (if intended) right to vote provided upon their conviction each one to forfeit a Ninety nine percent (99%) of the actual vote (so, one hundred terrorists vote to count one vote) for the remainder of their life. (There would be a freeze in voting between the act of terror performed and the conviction.

• Murderers to resume their constitutional (if intended) right to vote provided upon their conviction, each one to forfeit a Ninety-eight percentage (98%) of an actual vote.

Thereafter, they shall gain each year One percent (1%) of an actual vote, and upon good behavior the total of which shall not exceed 5% of an actual vote. There would be a freeze in voting between the act of murder performed and the conviction.

• Rapists to resume their constitutional (if intended) right to vote provided upon their conviction each one to forfeit Ninety seven percent (97%) of an actual vote. Thereafter, the release shall gain One Percent (1%) of an actual vote each year upon good behavior, the total of which not to exceed 5% of an actual vote. There would be a freeze in voting between the act of rape performed and the conviction.

• ………….. TBD by the Congress.

• ………….. TBD by the Congress.

• Illegal Immigrants to gain right to vote starting the day when if they're granted an alien number among with NSA's express approval provided the value of each not to exceed five percent (5%) of an actual vote during their good standing until they gain the status as a legal immigrant, having granted Green card.

• Legal Immigrants to gain the right to vote starting the day they're granted the actual approval and sworn as a legal alien provided the value of each not to exceed (75% of an actual vote or TBD by the congress) of an actual vote until they gain natural citizenship status.

• Naturalized Citizens to gain a right to vote starting the day they're sworn as a naturalized citizen provided the value of each vote not to exceed ninety five percent (95%) of an actual vote.

• American Born Citizen and Over five Years Naturalized Citizens to gain right to vote after a certain age, known the legal applicable age for American Born Citizens.

Effect: Such an Amendment places the nation's voting system in a realistic way closer to the intention of the Constitutional Frame-Path and Nation's Congressional best interest to bind the states to gain control over their status should it ever go unleashed.

23.
CORONA VIRUS

I.

Today is April 9th ,2020, the 24th day of a "One Month Stay at Home Precaution" that, American have practiced preventing this worldwide pandemic,

Persisting an unexpected number of death toll top, fifteen thousand only in the United State of America

there are thousands scientific and otherwise suggestions whether are given directly or otherwise to mitigate this epidemic.

The following is one of which the author hereby is suggesting:

Due to a possible presumption that, some of these infected patients were <u>Scared to Death</u> prior to a positive effect of medication when for the first time in their entire life seeing <u>everyone around their bed in the hospital have a scary mask,</u> would it make any difference should the doctors and nurses each to also wear a BIG SMILEY COLOR PICTURE of themselves (in a neckless form) underneath reads............THIS IS DCTOR...SO AND SO....

II.
THE LEGACY OF THIS CRONA VIRUS:

1.The **SOCIAL DISTANCING** is a temporary **legacy** that may lends to credence as a permanent **legacy** in some **parts** for the following major social groups of the following first category:

- Mega groups:

a) Education in any manners (probably not with many changes or social distancing)
b) Exercise of any kind (perhaps slight changes to support the health)
c) Preaching and praying (perhaps with changes to support the health)

- Smaller groups probably with changes in social distancing

a) Businesses
b) Labor

EFFECT: The **proper** social distancing and being **social** in an appropriate fashion sound to be the best elements in **civilization** in addition to secure the health. False tolls to abuse such as **equality in a wrongful manner** should not be **adhered** to either side to distancing advocates.

2. The attachment to the mask in the winter times shall foster a new preventive effect to any virus or bacteria's such as flue.

24.

THE ROLE OF THE DEHUMIDIFIER TO EXCLUDE VIRUS OF THE AIR

Dehumidifier takes the moisture in the form of liquid water off the air where in general contains different kinds of viruses.   By disposing the water, the chance of existence of such viruses be reduced or amounted to the zero. This shall function as a preventive device as to the ventilator being a treatment instrument.

25.

CORONAVIRUS THEORY

Would the human being be able to CURE this disease?

Should STRATEGY be a good way to cope with this pandemic?

Would the Bill Gate past funding thus, the United States recent one be enough for the CURE?

For the purpose,
While a success in the <u>DEVELOPED ERA</u> of the science hasn't been reached despite all appropriate efforts should we step back to scrutinize the <u>OLD TESTMENT</u> era? If so,

I

The author hereby informs his audience readers and researchers to **THE VOYNICH CODE** , the World's Mysterious Manuscript Secrets of the Nature years prior to the Davinci code and during the 14th Century era in a video clip where observed *PICTUR OF FLOWERS HAVING SIMILRITY TO THE CORONAVIRUS* in two occasions.

II

Considering the developed era on April 24th of the 2020 the president of the United States of America, Donald J. Trump has suggested the following *Wise Question in a form of following suggestions to the health and scientists on the duration of different times that Solar Energy should be able under certain temperature and humidity to destroy the Corona as well as other viruses on the metal surfaces in the open areas.   Comparing with chemicals such as Bleaches and Alcohol would do the same respectively in minutes and in a second.*

Q: An exercise of capability of Solar Energy on destruction of the Virus in the human body by means of injection (minimal invasive) presumed laser kind injection as a cure. Perhaps to the specific minimal area!

The author finds this suggested question interesting for any subsequent research provided the following criteria if to stand credence

- *The injection for the purpose to treat the infected patient.*
- *The injection, or any types of Solar Therapies for longer treatment of the infected patient.*
- *If the prior experienced example such as eye laser injections concerns Ultraviolet which is the electromagnetic process, <u>should it be a solid research of an Ultra TBD, Solar-magnetic process</u> to succeed the virus?   If so,*

For the recipient of such an injection to accept,
the (physical body expectation) of the Ultra TBD, Solar-magnetic injection is an issue then,
the psychology of recipient and the creature of the injection
is another issue as
the <u>Solar,</u> Sun being <u>a female</u> symbolically (see the following).

An analogy I remember forty years ago when in small town near clear Lake city of NASA called Woodland it was put in a referendum if the people could use (payless) Helicopter as a taxi going to work to Houston and return?

The people turned it down on the psychology of flying. Otherwise, we should now be having Air Taxi all over the land.

26.

A LEGAL INSTRUMENT

Despite all other chapters, this chapter was referenced from an actual old well known instrument that, I let you go through and gueSS WHAT! Then, at the end see the title.

- *We the undersigned, acting by the authority of German High Command, hereby surrender unconditionally to the Supreme Commander, Allied Expeditionary Forces and simultaneously to the Soviet High Command all forces on land, sea, and in the air who are at this date under German control.*

- *The German High Command will at once issue orders to all German military, naval, air authorities and to all forces under German control to cease active operations at……. 2301……. hours Central European time on …… 8 May …… and to remain in the position occupied at that time. No ship, vessel, or aircraft is to be scuttled or any damage done to their hull, machinery, or equipment.*
- *The German High Command will at once issue to the appropriate commanders and ensure the carrying out of any further orders issued by the Supreme commander, Allied Expeditionary force and by the Soviet High Command.*
- *This act of military Surrender is without prejudice to and will be superseded by any general instrument of surrender imposed by or on behalf of the United Nations and*

applicable to Germany and German armed forces as a whole.

- *In the event of the German High Command or any of the forces under their control failing to act in accordance with this act of surrender, the Supreme Commander, Allied Expeditionary Forces, and the Soviet High Command will take such punitive or other action as they deem appropriate.*

Signed at ……………… on the ………

…………………………………………………..
On behalf of the German High Command

IN THE PRESENCE OF

……………………………………………..
On behalf of the Supreme Command

……………………………………………………
……………………………………………...
Allied Expeditionary Forces

....

....

On behalf of Soviet High Command

So, the Title above to read as .... THE

ACT OF MILLITARY SURRENDER,
1945....

"Instrument of Surrender"

27.

SNORE THEORY

The definition:

Snore is the sound/S of the human breath vibration caused by an underlying built up stocked to the person's mixtures, liquid dried attached to the roof of the mouth and the nose's upper section.

28.

DIVORCE AND SOCIAL DISTANCING RULE

It's been experienced in several divorce cases while the control yet being in the hands of the couples prior to their separation each marriage life was sacrificed by a product called <u>procedure</u>, the aggression of each party or both (but not the real arguments, always being <u>essential)</u>. How this problem can be developed to help the couples? Years the marriage contract has introduced and recognized like a **business contract** rather being with a **Moral Contractual Prestigious**. If so, why shouldn't it to be using some of the positive contractual rules of business one of which such as " **Binding parties to a marriage contract shall**

exercise a written notice of divorce one month in advance to each other with a provision during which they should live together in a peaceful manner to satisfy a contractual divorce requirement (this allow them to peacefully in a relaxing atmosphere to consider circumstances during this month rather than a moment in aggression then divorce). This shall allow the business, capitalism, and morality all to supersede the aggression where consequentially decreases the rate in divorce.

29.

A FORGOTTEN LEGACY OF THE CIGARETTE

Considering both, positive and the negative aspects of the cigarette legacy the former as a supporter of a monster business has helped the economy and the latter as the destroyer of the health has placed the human non/smokers in danger regardless if any, being a relaxation for the smokers.

Here, the forgotten and an important legacy of the cigarette is **the burden that smokers to place on nonsmokers thus, they should be accountable!**

30.

BED AND THE CLOUD

Can we sleep comfortably and be safe on any bed kinds today?

Thought to ignore the clouds on their relationship with the atmosphere, stardust so, the space transmogrified events, yet we have not given a consideration to those humans made intel devices that requires **frequencies** to produce.

Frequency?   Do they travel through the human while sleeping on the **beds** and **mattresses** made of **metals**? And travel easier through the **metals** to the body?   Dose the human beings deserve to credence professional research on In/validity and outcomes of these questions? **Or simply go for an expense for the cost of replacement on beds made of totally wood then, the mattress of the memory foam.**

31

WAR…. NOW, THE PEACE

1. The **macro industries** grow both, materialistic and employment wise, numerical!

2. The **war industries** are a bigger of all the kinds.

3. It's too hard and almost **impossible*** to get rid of the war industry including its **employment** regardless the **wishes of entire peace related human industries**.

4. However, should it take time and efforts, it's possible to diminish a war industry's **destruction power** (not the industry itself) by **substitution** of **different industry/ies** like Space programs; that, would replace the materials of the equal costs the war materials where, the employment to remain to secure unemployment, numerical.

Not yet done!

Why numerical!

When you replace the employment, the **number of replacements** shouldn't only to match on echelon level then, the management **known as the signature approval investiture** but, it strongly is recommended the changes to include all levels in employment of the specific target war/s to **new** industry/ies

Now, you got the numerical!

If the numerical stays the same, then we don't incur unemployment catastrophes.

Should it ever happen if we only to diminish the **war material/s** in such industry (by the gun control amateur -opinion) and without regard to the **numerical employment**, a utopian policy then suggests, <u>**you are attempting to Kill jobs**</u>, many employments consequential to an unemployment catastrophe that, the numbers in loss may numerically be even higher than the loss numbers in a related war!

EFFECT: The author suggests that the above fact shall work to the best reliance to all **scientific facts** including one, known as the theology science, not superior to any at all.

*Remember, neither the author's audience readers nor the author shall be shifted any thought-burden on all the above difficulties because the **Numeric above** is too high and requires a burden-shift equal to the **world population**.

32.

SHOWERING THE HEAD WHILE THE HAIR

Now! I remember why my grand ma was holding me tide between her legs, used to be bath by her when I was three! This was the way she was preventing me to scape while her **NAILS** were **SLIGHTLY SCRATCHING** my **HEAD'S <u>SKINS</u>** so, the soap to have its maximum cleaning effect on head than the hair.

Yes,

She has intended or otherwise, she knew or not..............the **head** a protector and governing structure of the body, the brain is needed to **breath trough it's nerves skin slots.**

AND

One of the best possible way is to pursue with

the title of this chapter

but the scratch must be with the nail and very **Lightly then** to clean the nail.

EFFECTS:

Average age increase and the life convene!

Turtles advising the human "…. I protected my head under my shell to live 200 years…. (ref. vol.1 chapter 48).

33.
THE STORM

A few days ago, was about February the 15th when the Famous Snow of the year 2021 has covered the entire Texas, broken powers, no electricity, no heater, no water, no warm air, for two days then, more...., having no past historical record but Alaska. Ways below zero the temperature shapes solid hanging icicles in the house where I left all my water lines dripping on to prevent leaks. This included several lines in the walls being frozen then, broken a few as well under the house. This usually happens lightly in each normal winter but, not this time and causing pipes damages for most pear and beam houses in Texas. To survive these famous days, I remember having put my winter clothes and gloves on wearing a special hat showing nowhere on my face except my eyes and lips then hiding under the blankets and bedspread where I could convert my breath to a warm air to shape the only available natural heater for the entire forty-eight hours.

EMERGENCY TRAININGS

Among all the sad memories I've experimented was to stay clean like the International Space Station's Astronauts and using the Detergent Container, Grocery Bags, and Wet Napkins for Toilet and Bath Usages all of which if we had prior practice then, it would easily be practicable for the emergencies if not rushed upon **(or even to be used as a mid-night wake-up, you don't want to wake the other party)!** One more advice is while you're left without water lines then, it takes only a bottle of water for two weeks to clean your face (among respiratory cleaning thought for ordinary non-emergency situations as well) as follow: (a) Take a tissue (b) fold it three times (c) lightly wet it by 8 drips then, clean your Eyes   (d) take another tissue (e) fold it three times (f) pour to wet it again with 8 drips using your pinky finger to clean up the internal walls of your nose a few times. now, you even feel you can breathe easier than before.

NATION'S RELIEF PROJECT

Here is my Intuition to remedy the above dilemma A NEW WATER PIPELINE:
(1) To Manufacture new Copper Line bigger than the existing one that is internally attached-sealed

by another tiny copper line where runs hot water in a circuit from and to the water heater by a small motor for the frozen times (emergencies). Or
(2) To Manufacture and attach a motor to the top of water heater that runs only on frozen days as to (A)directs the water heater upper portion's (warm but not hot due to the circulation) water and distributing it to the entire house cold lines returning to the water heater prevents from freezing.
(B) Direct a secondary distributing line (original hot lines) from the bottom portion of the water heater (closed to the burner) without using that motor where it holds real hot water as usual!

EFFECT: A New Winter Dilemma Resolution.
The necessity of having professional engineering's design is a must!

34.

THE STRANGER

1. Among all the parental educations, we teach our kids
" stay off the strangers".
So,
**they stay off, also off of <u>the strangers who weren't
intended too</u>!**

2. Starting from pre k then, the upper levels I've
experienced that, the teachers do the
    same advise in the different manners consistent to
the age of the recipient.
    Yet, **they stay off, both groups while the cognizance
to the latter becomes hard**
    without an attachment seeking their help.

    This to become more complex when they reach to
    the Generation Z age then, new employees.
The teachers, being the big kids continue the same
advice to the new generation of all.

**The big kids of all generations now, in their status
being employees are less trusted to the other groups,**

Known the employers
 because
    Yet,
they stay off both group-strangers
the complex now,
is a dilemma!
    They cannot be in a group or trust a group more than
the one themselves have shaped!
    or
IT'S BEEN SHAPED FOR THEM!

    "The Strangers of both kinds being everywhere"!

To resolve this dilemma shaping it in the favor of the humanity:

1. It's needed "***Categorizing the Cognizance of the mistaken strangers who were not intended in the first place" from the Age pre-k up to the end in elementary school.***
2. ***Thereafter,***
   The cognizance is strength.

35.

PREVENTIVE OF THE DISASTERS, THE NATION'S RELIEF PROJECT

The Storm Disaster of the Texas in February of the 2021 is well known to Texans however, other states citizens were living with their ordinary and normal course of life routine!

When one or two states to face such a disaster, should a Federal Policy to exist?

If so,

Ten, here the following Policy Projection may be a

partial remedy to this dilemma:

1. The Social Security Cards to have the appearance of the following changes on their face without any change to their actual legal status

(a) appearance of the **person's photo**.

(b) a change on the **quality** of the card, being plastic like credit cards.

(c) having a ***secondary number* categorizes the nation** by their domicile; regional, local, and statewide.

(d) any **other changes** lend to credence then ,TBD the **US Congress**

2. In event of a **regional** disaster if to incur **locally or state wise**, the government to **apply** a **DISASTER RELEIF FUND** only to the effected citizens of that region prior ***to their life being endangered.***

THUS,
THEIR SECONDARY NUMBERS TO BE ACTIVATED A CERTAIN DISASTER-AMOUNT TO CREDIT SIMILAR TO THE FOOD STAMP CARD.

36.

SPECIAL CRISTAL FOR LAPTOP

Should a laptop be used under the sun light, either it is hard to see the screen, or it will be damaging the eyes!

To have this as a **necessity** enriched, the question calls if a modification on laptop's **Cristal** is needed to fulfill the purpose?

THE EFFECT OF MODIFICATION: To have extra visual access then, to secure the eye in both, under the sun for the daily life and the intelligence forces usage of our troops.

37.

THE BEDTIME ICE WATER

To keep the bedtime water cold the entire night to the morning like the champagne in its bucket

should be very easy, isn't it?

Just have your bottle of water in the freezing compartment of the refrigerator half an hour before the sleeping time or to a frozen point having yet half the water. This to stay cool to the morning.

38.
MECHANICAL BULLS

A few chapters of the volume 1. of this book are concerned then, effective with efforts to increase the average age of all interested persons however, this one has a specific effect, and it works on individual who are **over eighty years of age, over weighted, disabled, or otherwise are lazy and for some reason/s they can't walk enough to *digest their foods,*** an essential element of the existentialism. **The following Business Proposal   shall help The Nation of the above categories to   Gain a Greater   access   to their lives   extending it while they are deemed to be deserved upon!**

Probably you've heard What a Mechanical Bull is?

You see it mostly in front of some grocery stores for kids to sit and ride on it!

The Cowboy in Texas uses it for the ride training on cows!

Then, is it the time?

The designers and manufactures to Combine the <u>mechanism</u> of mechanical bull with the health Club's Bicycle making a New Product capable with and controllable by motion speed to be **used for the purpose intended above** provided the speed of its movement to follow a standard health criterion where to be ready for the sellers to place it in the market **private and public facilities**.

Here, while the actual mechanical bulls already have their name chosen so, the health club bikes, then, should a new name like

"Life Extension Pedal" to satisfy this?

Effect: Hopping to round up the average age if not to the 100, then why not to the 90?

39.

REWARD AND AWARD

The later requires no return in exchange while the former dose! Here the award gives or orders to give something as an official payment, compensation, or prize and without a return while the reward is given for the recognition of one's service, effort, or achievement.
However, both are possessed by a

FORGOTTEN

Important issue,

A LEGAL ACCEPTANCE.

There should be a legal acceptance like the acceptance of
an offer in a valid CONTRACT
So, to prevent us to a blind acceptance!
It's never weighted such! Why?

The FRAMERS always intentionally or if otherwise, mistakenly, or incapably wanted to lower the intel-human
POWER OF EXPENDITURE to supersede over.
(This shall preclude those to whom a reward and award deemed a necessity!)

40.

BABIES RIGHT

It's on or around May 2021. The most medias are
reflecting to exaggerate one news only,

" The New baby Girl's name",

one of the British monarch new arrivals

The parents, Meghan and Harry are in the state of
insistence to have the baby called

"Lilibet Diana".

on the other hand, the medias unanimously are
relating this as an "INSULT to the Queen".
Here while the author releases himself of any
political analysis of the issue then, having the only
concern on:

"A LEGAL RIGHT OF BABIES"!

the SENERIO TO FOLLOW…..
It is the 2025……. But, not any reflection yet! …

It is the 2027......when the baby's school atmosphere calls   the name NOW, A seven-year-old don't like to hear…. Oh, not suitable?

Thereafter,

And beyond the 2027, now she is a teen,

more HUMILIATING?

Who knows the reflection on such a name while in adulthood?

EFFECT: The audience readers reasonably may now claim to establish Babies Legal Rights to their parents.

41.

A CORONAVIRUS LEGACY

When the mask be precluded everywhere then, shall it be kept enforced to the last Three Isles areas of the Home Depot where covers the sale of Concrete, Brick, and Woods for the sake of **purchasers** and their **employees**?

EFFECT: The general health

42.

NONSTOP TALKING

I remember when having my second shot of Covid 19,

the nurse has asked the following question then,

one of my intuitive answers I've ever experienced in my life was!

Q. "Did you have any reaction on your first vaccine"?

A. "Yes!   sever!   five hours!   Nonstop talking Chinese"!

43.
RENOVATION
TO DECREASE THE DIVORCE RATE

When a married couple who are tired of each other while they've lived together in one place of residence for a long time an important question that they're faced with, is,

Dose the primary scope of this tiredness is based upon the **environmental circumstances** that, lends to credence the **unleashed separation**.

So, to prevent the divorce

the Old Rule of Thumb always may not work, as it suggests an Involvement Having more Children around
is a security to the relationship.

Therefore,

a **renovation** creates a superior involvement in marriage especially the renovation connected to a **change in a place of living** that, consequentially changes the new neighbors (who may have been the direct cause of the divorce).

EFFECT: A "lifetime lasting Marriage", isn't this what we always wanted?

44

NOT A GENERATION SILENT

Should we ever to ask any member in generation Z, Millennial and or the Baby boomer they all and simultaneously **define** the **Generation Silent** being of **those who were born prior to the age of the baby boomers**.

A study also reveals all the **four generations are named** somehow as **to their respective times of their existence.**

Here, the **concern is** on the **framer's wrong selection** of their name and **only** as to the **Generation Silent**, a generation that, **has the most** and **effective** VOICES OF ALL THE TIMES even more than the other generations then, **everywhere**. For example, **in Constitution** - as to the **George Washington** (he is everywhere with the last three generations and reflective to their every days live), the same **in Law** - as to the **Marbury or Maddison**, **to the Art** - as to the **Leonardo da Vinci** ... and so on.... **even the ordinary people (the silence goes) to** an attachment to their **alive families** ....

So, why the generation SILENCE ?

Do the ADVOCATES want/ed us to have more
RELIANCE to?
The OUT GONER/S

and to forget about

those whose GENES ARE THE PRODUCTS OF
THE
NEWER INTEL HEREDITY, the new commers

So, the most in our nation sooner to approach
to the grave? or it's best to advocate the
average age increase by

CHANGE IN THE NATION'S ROLE EXPECTANCY

AMONG WITH EACH
Newer generation/s, THE GENERATION
EXISTENTIAL!

they want to explore beyond

and one of which is,

GOING THROUGH THE SPACE….

45

THE EASY WAY VIRUS
PRECAUTION AND PREVENTION

1. Is the hand washing good-only?
2. Any time when you get home of a longer than a
   two hours outside-trip/s then, the following
   strategies are the best to practice while
   A smell-sensed virus of any kind may have
   then, sticked to the FACE or across the
   INTERNAL NOSE WALL,
   persisting to enter
   especially when you recognize that smell, the
   allergy

   (a) It sounds to be very easy! only it takes **two**
       extra minutes longer while hand washing
       then,
   (b) **(1) Soap-wash your face and your nose's**
       Internal Walls with your kidney finger
       Or easier way!
   (b)**(2) BUY WET KNAPKIN OF THE "DOLLAR**
           THREE" AND PRACTICE the (b)(2)
   REMEMBER! This should off even a simple cold
   virus! (also, see chapter 24)
   Info. Essential, Some viruses grew well in the
       hot air while others in the cold. That is why
       the Covid vaccines are kept ways below the
       zero temperature.

46.

TOILET SPLASHES

Should ever be used an outside toilet rather than the one at home,
It would have sounded some being too angry when the flash water pressure goes beyond the norm splashing it up!

Are we safe?

Physicians unanimously are with an opinion that,

"it's a serious source to spread Related Viruses to the user. "

EFFECT: Keep then, a half standing position while flashing!

47.

NATURALLY CONDITIONED AIR BY OR WITHOUT AIR CONDITION

In the September then, the October the state of Texas and some other regions often to reach the smoothest air of the year.

Is there a preference usage on the natural air rather than, conditioned by the air condition?

Can we modify the divisive function of the Air condition where we only to get the **natural air** rather than the internally circuited air and by the air condition?

Yes, we can do it,

Mechanism Cognizance:

A) A ceiling fan in the house deals only with the air inside the house with no regard to the change of its **condition** unless the air condition is on or when the entrance door and windows are open or the external walls to influence the internal walls by the outside changes in temperature.

A) When the air condition's internal fan is on **only**, it also deals with the air inside the house limited to the internal flexible foil ducts and the closed-circuit air inside the house.

MODIFICATION ON THE AIR CONDITION SYSTEM TO USE THE OUTSIDE AIR WHEN SMOTH AND DESIRABLE:

A) When we turn the air condition thermostat to the off position then, only to turn on The Fan Switch there exists no outside air to travel inside the ducts then, the house unless

A) Installment of **A New DEVICE** to convert the outside air,

a newly be invented an internal valve

The function:

{It opens and closes a roof or eaves slot into the attic's flexible foil duct (using an extended duck) directing the outside natural air-in with a small fan.}

EFFECT: Regional usage in the areas where the natural weather has a long cooling duration within two to six months of the year then, results utility savings in addition to the natural consumption.

48.

THE BEST LEGACY OF THE COVID 19

Among several legacies the Coronavirus has left behind one has the best consequential
survival effect…….

Yes……., We've never used Optional Winter Masks in the past to Prevent A SIMPLE COLD VIRUS!
Where and when we feel the allergy
Dose the winter mask helps to save us regardless the Covid?

Here is,
the actual exaggerated story.

In the past and prior to the Covid 19, **every year in fact we did have too many winter deaths* from the regular flue, and other related cold viruses though yet not well recognized. The number* was high too but <u>it has never showed up**</u> since it was hidden by a crowd known as the three hundred million! <u>So, the number always perceived normal</u>, and there always Lacked <u>a Power Reduction Efforts</u> for the time being until appearance of the interested persons, Bill Gate or Donald Trump.**

Also, there has existed no **PANIC*, DANGER*, MEDIA* and or EXAGGERATION*** at the time.

Then, the beginning of the Covid Cognizance though the known incident being true it's followed by **the exaggerations, propagandas, techs, and the BIG BOYS' ADVANTAGES,** what It has never been shown **……. **is Now** showing*.
Now!!!,
Can we use the

Winter Mask Optional?

If to be known a

legacy 19

where to help to decrease the actual number* that, always has existed?

It sounds being practical!

Being on-masked for the winter or when is required by the employer also limits the

in-take oxygen

specially for the kids

Then, the mask rule may be changed to justify,

A face place position, UNDER THE NOSE

or if practicable then,

The Mask itself to be replaced

By

something you can breathe easier

The author's Newly Patent Project,

SWIMMING CAP

It lock-tides under the chin and above the nose leaving two small open hole slots up-around the nose to breathe with a demeanor look likes clown's nose being longer where with inhale- exhale it opens and closes then, releases-out the carbon dioxide of those hole slots while exhaled. It doesn't require ear tie elastic strap around and capable of being cleaned by alcohol then, be reused again.

49

STAND SLEEPING

Stand sleeping is the astronautical engineering of our sleeping fashion out of the atmosphere, and in the space then, probably it is equipped with a safety Jacket tide to the standing bed positioned to hold the head and body norm.

Stand Sleeping *and*
Jacket-tide up-beds *are the products of space enrichment that may give us discretionary clue to go beyond our normal space usage to the,*

Atmospheric Developments!

And its Anticipatory **purposes**

to develop Periodic or whole Night Sleep for those who are in needs to change their flat sleeping inability position due to the circumstances such as their system maldigestions!

SHOULD IF THEN TO BE USED IN HOSPITAL,

Intense Care Units?

Or may ordinarily be used at home if it works in case the person producing much alarming gas during the flat sleeping times, so while in upright position the relief to support the care.

The health Professionals may also modify to reposition this equipment for therapeutical treatment.

even the developments in sciences are the products of THE GENERATION AFTER!

50.
KIND AND AGGRASIVE

Be kinder than **necessary**

Because,

everyone you meet these days is involved with
some kinds of Battles!

51

DOUBLE DISHWASHER

TO SUGGEST A COMFORT ZONE IN CONNECTION TO THE
DISHWASHING A THEORY SUGGESTS AS FOLLOW BUT, REQUIRES
EFFORTS BY DESIGNERS, MANUFACTURERS AND THE SELLERS:

1) INSTEAD OF ONE, THERE ARE TWO DISHWASHERS
2) BOTH ARE ATTACHED TO A SINGLE MOTOR
3) THE SIZE OF EACH IS SMALLER THAN THE ACTUAL SIZE
    PENDING UPON THE CHARACTERISTIC OF THE HOUSE.
4) **THERE WOULD BE NO EXTRA WORK TO TAKE THE DISHES
    OUT INTO THE CABINET**
5) **ONE OF THE PROPOSED DISHWASHER FUNCTIONS AS A
    CABINET WHILE THE OTHER RUNS TO WASH**
6) IF TO BUY A NEW HOUSE, THE COST MAKES NO
    DIFFERENCE WHILE BEING FINANCED
7) SHOULD YOU INTEND TO REPLACE FOR YOUR EXISTING
    RESIDENT THEN, THE BURDEN OF THE EXTRA COST
    SHOULDN'T EXCEED THE LONG-RANGE COMFORT
    ZONE WHEN YOU HAVE IT INSTALLED.

EFFECT: CREATES EXTRA JOBS IN ALL THE THREE INDUSTRIES
         AND A REAL COMFORT FOR THE HOUSE OWNERS.

52.

PRESIDENTIAL ELECTION

In its background, this chapter of the volume one, (hereby exactly appears in the following) has revealed the author's assertion that**, …. "The prior occupation of the past presidents is the most effective and influential element to the nation's lifestyle within and somehow after the scope of such presidency"** …….

if to only consider the paragraph in this chapter quote, where the words start with ………perhaps the candidate Donald Tru…….

then,

the writer's position regarded one of the Candidate Trump's prior occupations, as **"being a billionaire" whereas this** hasn't totally credence his guess and instead,

what the American people have experienced was,

The effects in the Candidate's prior secondary occupation,

"Apprentice Producer"

Was at stake,

And being beyond an ordinary scope,

Designed professionally,
and skilled desirably

then,

everywhere……

in White House meetings
conferences,
in with campaign audiences,
and even through the pre-arranged impeachment.

SHOUD IF HE GOES FOR THE SECOND TERM,

**Perhaps the first writer's guess then, to become
The true….**

In the August of 2016 the following chapter as an article has appeared on Facebook while the chapter 13 of the volume one reflects this as follow in 2019

THE PRESIDENTIAL ELECTION AN IMPARTISAN THEORETICAL OPINION

• Background:
  An overall analysis shows that the prior occupations of the past presidents

were the most effective and influential element to the American people

lifestyle within the scope of the presidency as to the following evidence:

• A soldier as a president, Gen. Eisenhower had an effect of war to most
of the people.

• A religion-minded opportunity had only been the people choice in politics
and otherwise, political, social, and even economical aspects of our nation and nations at large during the President, Jimmy Carter Administration.

- President Ronald Reagan era had the most characteristics effects of movie producers.

- President Bill Clinton has been so involved with the people into the legality whereas himself being an evident in the cases involving Monica Lewinsky and Paula Jones while a European magazine has quoted his impeachment "the commencement era of organized school kid killers as the news cover up shield"

- President George Bush, the father, brought the intelligence, thus the son business.
- Not only the prior occupation of the presidents but, the proper or even
improper nominal powers of the people mostly were gained by a partial system necessity such as nominal admissions to the law schools as to Curtis, Justin, and Marshals or even names associated with "Bomb" or "Obey Mama" so, to help in prevention of terrorists to bomb or kill the people.

- Perhaps the candidate, Donald Trump may help the people, if not to become
milliners then, to be relieved of their financial difficulties. Both, the people

with less than four digits' bank figures and the people between four to eleven digits while their difficulties are equal, the same with a different class rank.

This shall fashion an ultimate rich minded generation of real capitalism.

• Female as a president in the United States:
European, second and the third
world countries most have experienced female leaders within the scope of

 presidency or kingdom while having placed more than thousands of years of

 experiences. The United States with 300 years yet being so young to have

a female leader because if to consider a consequential side effect in the

nation as to the sacrificial percentage of females within the scope of a female

leadership compared to the male leadership, the best theory suggests

no consequential increase is needed in the female sacrifice. Therefore,

a Utopian advocacy theory shall stand for the best interest of the people the United States to start its female leadership experience first within

the scope of a Vice Presidency only to prevent a high female sacrifice, both at

home and abroad.

53.
SHOUD THE QUEEN TO HONOR,
REGARDLESS TO WHOM THE CROWN BE
GRANTED A GAIN

The British nation with all the proven dignities is deserved to crown the one, the most to servitude!

Here is a nation with a seven decades of record-breaking leadership!

Is this the Queen?

Should it have happened if a King?

Oh, No! No!

The leading was supported then, the strength of which was created to back-bone the British Stone-layers by and through a term known, "Femaleship".

A term stands as in **biblical** a definition for the God's characteristics!

And to stand in **Britannia**, a definition for the **Britain**!

The **Sun** and **Moon** having the same designation!

EFFECT: IT ONLY SOUNDS,
If not a **Cost Prohibitive** then, it's <u>**Costly**</u> **for a nation to move to the other direction, should if not for the DEFINITION!**

54.

THE DRIVING GLOVES

IT IS OFTEN USED AS A FASHION AND ALWAYS BEEN DESIGNED TO SATISFY THIS PURPOSE. AS A RESULT, MOST OF THE PAST MARKET- DEMANDS WERE AMONG THE YOUNGER GENERATIONS.

IT APPEARS NOW THE **AGED GROUPS** ARE THE TARGET DEMAND WHILE HAVING THE FOLLOWING BODY DEFICIENCIES AMONG WHICH THE FOLLOWINGS ARE THE MOST NEEDED ATTENTION ONES:

1) HAND ISSUES AND PROBLEMS
2) HAND AND JOINT ISSUES
3) HAND NERVE CLEAN UP NECESSITY
4) WREST ISSUES
5) ....

THOUGHT, A NECESSITY REQUIRES THIS GENERATION DRIVE TO SURVIVE THUS,

THE USE OF **CERTAIN DESIGNED AND MANUFACTURED GLOVES** MAY HELP THEM WHILE THE FOLLOWING TO BE OF THE IMPORTANCE:

"WHEELS OF NEW CARS ARE PRODUCING NO VIBRATION TO THE STEERING WHEELS" IS OF A WRONG OPINION HOWEVER,

ROADS LACK THE 2050-QUALITY-SMOOTHNESS AND WHEN YOU DRIVE REGARDLESS THEN, YOU FEEL THE NOISE OF THE ROAD, **AS A CONTINUES SOUND-VIBRATION ON THE STEERING WHEEL.** THIS INCURS MOST OFTEN AND **WITHOUT NOTICE** CAUSING PROBLEM TO THE **AGED GROUPS** WHILE THEIR HANDS ARE BEING WITH A LESSER-NERVE-STRENGTH.

THEREFORE,

NOT THE ONE ALREADY FASHION DESIGNED BUT,
A PROPOSED RELATIVE-MATERIAL SPECIFICALLY MANUFACTURED FOR THE PURPOSE THEN, DESIGNED TO SATISFY **A VIBRATION** REDUCTION TEST MAY LEND TO CREDENCE THIS PROJECT.

EFFECT: LESSER PAINS FOR THIS CREATURE OF OTHER GENERATIONS THEN, **THE AVERAGE** AGE INCREASE.
OH BY THE WAY I HAVE CROSSED BY A GLOVE IN CVS YESTERDAY THAT ALMOST LENDS TO CREDENCE CALLED, COPPER FIT.

55.
ALL RIGHTS RESERVED

This title mostly been viewed on copyright page at the beginning of the most published books,

TO WHOM IS IT RESERVED TO?

WHO IS IN FACT RESERVING IT?

It's true that, no author has an intention to reserve, nor it is an **informed consent** of an author, while they have no clue as to the actual LEGAL **RESERVATION OF THE RIGHTS** instead, they are **repetitive of the words**, All Rights Reserved or they take it easy.

Here are the three groups,

1.   The author, most of whom a monetary capability of using their works for the rights of the nation are limited to zero.

   3.   All the groups' investors but not limited to the interest group and individual investors, who

have more monetary capability than the author to pursue the author's work for the right of the nation but, **they fear of the reservation**.

3. <u>**The wrong sides of the tech, then, the connections beyond**</u> who in fact are the advocates of the title to Keep it locked to the intellectuals and intelligences as a risk to their interest.

EFFECT: The first group shall never monetary be capable to servitude the nation with their works as the **capitalism requires capitals**.
It sounds, a long-time practice of a-routine-mistake, not to have the second group involvement in and by the capitalism then, to be risky!

EFEECT: Right side of the intellectualism so, intelligence would have a light effect to the otherwise.

CAN I ASK YOU A FAVOR?

If you enjoyed this book, please post a short review on Amazon. Your support really does make a difference and I value your feedback.

If you'd like to leave a review, please use the amazon link below:

Link

Thanks again for your support!

ABOUT THE AUTHOR

Frank Hiri taught and practiced real estate among with well-known companies in Texas whereas simultaneously he taught as a substitute teacher at high, middle, and elementary schools. Previously, Frank worked as an acting, then assistant consul at the Imperial Consulate General of Iran in Houston, Texas prior to the Islamic Revolution. He completed equivalent graduate courses in education and law to two doctoral programs while holding a master's degree in Public Administration and a BA in Political Sciences. He then, received a high qualified teaching certificate in Social Studies. Frank is a self-motivated and an innovative thinker. He consistently pursues new challenges to stretch abilities, expand knowledge to bring a greater return.

Made in the USA
Columbia, SC
04 July 2022

62716218R00065